LIFE IN AMERICA 100 YEARS AGO

Health and Medicine

LIFE IN AMERICA 100 YEARS AGO

Health and Medicine

Law and Order

Manners and Customs

Rural Life

Transportation

Urban Life

Health and Medicine

DAVID RITCHIE
AND FRED ISRAEL

Chelsea House Publishers

New York   Philadelphia

CHELSEA HOUSE PUBLISHERS

Editorial Director: Richard Rennert
Executive Managing Editor: Karyn Gullen Browne
Copy Chief: Robin James
Picture Editor: Adrian G. Allen
Art Director: Robert Mitchell
Manufacturing Director: Gerald Levine
Assistant Art Director: Joan Ferrigno

LIFE IN AMERICA 100 YEARS AGO
Senior Editor: Jake Goldberg

Staff for **HEALTH AND MEDICINE**
Assistant Editor: Annie McDonnell
Designer: Lydia Rivera
Picture Researcher: Sandy Jones
Cover Illustrator: Steve Cieslawski

3 5 7 9 8 6 4 2
Library of Congress Cataloging-in-Publication Data

Ritchie, David
     Health and medicine/David Ritchie and Fred Israel.
         p. cm.—(Life 100 years ago)
     Includes bibliographical references and index.
     ISBN 0-7910-2839-9
     1. Medicine—United States—History—19th century—Juvenile literature.
     [1. Medicine—History.] I. Israel, Fred L. II. Title. III. Series.
R151.R58 1994   94-17793
610'.973'09034—dc20   CIP
                                                                                      AC

CONTENTS

Health and Medicine

MEDICINE AND THE CIVIL WAR

NINETEENTH-CENTURY AMERICAN MEDICINE NOW SEEMS almost as unfamiliar to us as that of the Middle Ages. The medical profession of our day would be all but unrecognizable to the doctors of Abraham Lincoln's era. The typical physician of our time operates out of a hospital or office with a vast array of high-tech equipment. Modern therapeutics and technology have provided cures for illnesses that would have been considered sentences of death a hundred years ago. Drugs have defeated once-lethal infections. Some scourges of the past century, such as yellow fever, typhoid fever, and malaria, have virtually vanished from the modern industrialized world. Now anesthesiology— once a matter of dribbling ether onto a cloth placed over a patient's face—is a complex discipline in its own right, and surgeons use technologies ranging from the time-honored knife and needle to fiber optics and magnetic resonance imaging. All these advances would have seemed pure fantasy in the early to middle 19th century.

A typical doctor's office in Seattle in 1912.

Likewise, from our viewpoint, it is difficult to imagine what medicine was like in the days of our great-grandparents. It was rudimentary, risky, and painful. When 19th-century novelists wrote about fictional doctors with names like Fillgrave and Sawbones, they reflected a popular view of doctors and medicine that had much basis in fact. In many instances, doctors and their therapies probably were as dangerous as the diseases the physicians aimed to treat.

Much of what we consider modern medicine had not even been imagined in the mid-19th century. The doctor's pharmacopoeia, or choice of medications, was not much bigger then than in Shakespeare's day. In many situations where a modern physician could restore a patient to health with ease, the 19th-century doctor was helpless. There were no antibiotics. Surgery was primitive at best. Anesthesia consisted of a few drops of chloroform, or perhaps a good long swig of whisky before the surgeon started cutting. The danger from infected surgical incisions was tremendous, because doctors were just starting to understand the mechanisms of infectious disease. Modern aseptic procedure, which prevents infection by maintaining a sterile environment for surgery, had not been invented yet.

Unlike the modern hospital, that source of hope for suffering patients today, the 19th-century hospital was usually a place of dread, seen as a brief last stop on the way to the cemetery. Until the late 19th century, the hospital was barely more than a warehouse for the seriously ill and may have hastened the deaths of many patients by making the sick even sicker.

The 19th century marks the boundary, in many respects, between ancient and modern medicine. More specifically, one might place the dividing line between the old and modern eras of American medicine in the four-year period of the Civil War, from 1861 to 1865. The war created special medical needs and gave doctors abundant data and experience that led to great advances in American medical care after the Confederate surrender at Appomattox. Before the war, medical practice in America was almost medieval in character; after the war, change accelerated at a rapid rate.

11

Frontier doctors set up shop wherever they could, often in shacks, sod houses, or dugouts. In 1889, Doctors Eagleson and Smith set up their practice in a tent after a fire destroyed much of Seattle, Washington.

The Civil War was the bloodiest conflict in American history, and in some ways it was much more harmful to individual soldiers than warfare today. The soft lead bullets of the 1860s, for example, spread out and caused hideous wounds when they struck the body. By contrast, modern steel-jacketed bullets are more likely to leave relatively small, neat holes. Civil War bullets simply made hamburger, so to speak, of whichever part of the body they struck. As a result, virtually all penetrating wounds in the chest or abdomen were fatal.

Soldiers fared better when wounded in the arm or leg, but wounds there had a high mortality rate too, even if someone managed to carry the wounded man to a hospital. Such rescue was by no means assured. There were, as a rule, no ambulances to haul the wounded off the battlefield. In many instances, badly wounded soldiers simply were left to die where they fell.

It would be hard to say which prospect terrified soldiers more: slow death by exposure on a battlefield or the horrors of a field hospital. A field hospital had to treat vast numbers of casualties. Compassion and gentleness were not high priorities. Some anesthetics were available, but aseptic conditions were not. Surgeons wore coats stained with blood and pus. Surgical instruments and surgeons' hands were not disinfected. Moreover, doctors at the outset of the war tended to have little experience in surgery. Because medical education was generally poor, the so-called surgeon at a field hospital early in the war might be merely a glorified butcher, or worse. An ordinary butcher at least had some experience carving up hogs and cattle.

Grim statistics tell the story. Union soldiers with gunshot wounds in the chest had a mortality rate of more than 60 percent. In other

13

Early-20th-century pharmacists became merchants and dispensers of a variety of herbs, patent medicines, and "sure cures" that were supposed to provide instant relief, as well as confections and cosmetics. This picture shows the Silvernail Drugstore in Marietta, Minnesota, around 1910. In addition to the apothecary jars, note the Edison phonograph cylinders, a political poster for William Howard Taft, and an advertisement for Danderine, guaranteed to grow hair. Incidentally, the first American telephone exchange on record, built in 1877, linked a Hartford, Connecticut, pharmacy with 21 local doctors. The first telephone line in Rochester, Minnesota, set up in 1879, connected the farmhouse of Dr. William Mayo with the downtown drugstore.

A drugstore in Trinidad, Colorado, in 1880.

words, two out of every three soldiers with such wounds died. Abdominal wounds were even worse. More than 85 percent of such patients died. By contrast, more than 95 percent of Americans wounded during World War II survived. Overall, perhaps 10 percent of all Union troops and 15 percent of all Confederate soldiers died of wounds.

15

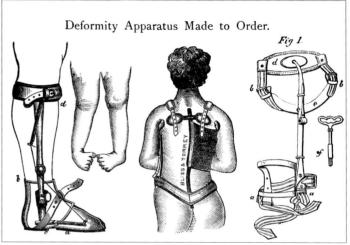

Deformity Apparatus Made to Order.

Medical and dental splints, made from thin copper, as well as special shoes and surgical apparatuses, were sold through the mail. These graphic ads represented the latest medical equipment available 100 years ago.

When Civil War soldiers could be treated for their wounds and survived the surgery itself, other potential killers were waiting. One was tetanus, in which toxins produced by a common bacterium caused muscles to contract. In many cases, the infected person died in agony, as his tightening muscles pulled his body into an archlike configuration and eventually halted breathing. Gangrene took its toll of lives too.

Such illnesses killed many hospital patients in the Civil War because doctors of the time had a poor understanding of infections. It was known that carbolic acid could be used to reduce the potential for infections. Civil War doctors, however, did not understand that contaminated instruments transmitted infections and needed to be sterilized. Filthy instruments were allowed to spread infection to soldiers' wounds. Doctors also seemed unaware that such infections had to be prevented before they started. Physicians mistakenly thought that the right procedure was to treat a wound with carbolic acid after an infection developed, not before. As a result, many infections were well advanced—and the patient doomed—by the time doctors got around to washing wounds with carbolic acid.

Much of the problem in such cases was ignorance of bacteriology. When wounded soldiers were dying by the thousands of infected wounds in Civil War hospitals, the great early advances in knowledge of bacteria and how they cause disease were still a few years in the future. Not until after the Civil War were the bacterial causes of many common diseases established.

This ignorance of bacteriology caused tremendous health problems for Civil War soldiers outside the hospital as well as inside it. Disease is thought to have killed some 250,000 Union soldiers and 164,000 Confederates during the war. The average soldier was ill several

The typical 19th-century frontier physician. Anyone claiming to be a physician could practice medicine on America's 19th-century frontier. These hearty men rode horseback, slept on the ground, crunched through winter forests on snowshoes, and forded swollen spring rivers. The pharmacy was in their saddlebag. They set broken limbs, bound wounds, delivered babies, and fought smallpox and pneumonia. Their cures were improvised, often crude.

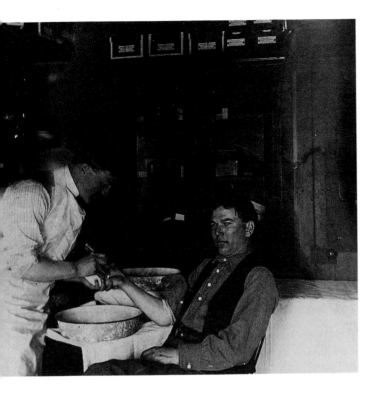

A cowboy has his hand treated in the office of a frontier doctor in Cambria, Wyoming, in 1890.

times per year. Poor sanitation and contaminated water spread such diseases as typhoid, dysentery, and diarrhea in the soldiers' camps. Malaria was a killer, as were respiratory infections such as tuberculosis and pneumonia. Gastroenteritis, inflammation of the stomach and intestinal tract, was yet another problem. It was aggravated by the soldiers' wretched diet of biscuits, beans, and salt beef, as well as the common practice of frying all foods. Stomach upsets were commonplace. Even scurvy—the painful, debilitating illness in which a deficiency of vitamin C causes teeth to loosen, gums to bleed, and old wounds to reopen—was widespread in the

19

camps: some 13 cases of scurvy occurred per 1,000 soldiers. The bottom line was that in the Civil War, diseases attributable to poor diet and ignorance of public hygiene were as dangerous as enemy bullets and bayonets.

Troops on the whole appear to have been healthier on the Union side than among the Confederates. Mortality rates from disease were considerably higher for Confederate troops than for Union soldiers. Various explanations have been proposed for this difference in mortality rates. Lack of medical supplies appears to have been one factor. The Southern troops, accustomed to a warm climate, also may have suffered more than Union forces from cold weather.

Rank was reflected in mortality patterns. Officers were more likely to die in battle, but illness was more likely to kill enlisted men. Race affected mortality rates, too. Among white Union forces, disease killed about 15 troops in every 1,000. Black troops fared worse. They fell ill and died in greater numbers than whites—perhaps five times as many where lung infections were involved.

Civil War medicine also suffered from a peculiar narrowness of concern on the part of doctors. Physicians appear to have had little awareness of what we would call the "whole patient." Today, doctors recognize that many different systems of the body, as well as the patient's attitude, may play vital roles in treating disease. That knowledge had yet to influence medical care in the Civil War, or if doctors were aware of it, then conditions in field hospitals gave them little or no opportunity to put it into practice.

To doctors in the early 1860s, a leg wound was a leg wound, and that was that. There was no recognition that recovery might depend on how well other parts of the body, such as the kidneys, performed. Patch him up and move on—that was the doctor's unwritten

An 1840 print illustrating an itinerant doctor selling his "liver medicine." Alcohol, as high as 100 proof, and herbs were the principal ingredients of these cures.

motto. The perception that he was treated as merely a piece of meat, to be chopped and perhaps sewn up afterward, must have made a profound impression on the mind of many a wounded soldier. One can only wonder how many wounded troops died from the impersonal, heartless attitude of their alleged healers.

By modern standards, the diagnostic equipment of mid-19th-century doctors was crude. The flexible stethoscope, which allows the physician to listen closely to a patient's breathing and heartbeat, was available as early as 1839, but such a simple and essential tool as the modern clinical thermometer was not developed until 1870. Early versions of such thermometers had to

21

be kept in contact with the patient for up to 25 minutes to obtain an accurate temperature reading.

After the Civil War, new discoveries led to great advances in public health and the treatment of individual patients. Wartime experience in running field hospitals, for example, was applied to civilian hospitals to make them more efficient. Postwar discoveries in microbiology had a dramatic effect on medicine and public health. Bacteria were recognized to be the cause of diseases such as cholera, diphtheria, tuberculosis, and typhoid fever. Assaults on disease at this level—bacteria and their mechanisms of transmission—paid off magnificently. At the same time, social and political structures emerged that allowed the modern hospital to develop, along with what we call the medical establishment.

The nightmares of wartime hospitals marked the end of the old era in American medicine. By war's end, the modern era was opening. It would have its own struggles and traumas, but nothing comparable to the dreadful four-year war that marked its beginning.

THE RISE OF
AMERICA'S HOSPITAL SYSTEM

THE HOSPITAL AS AMERICANS KNOW IT TODAY IS A RECENT invention. It did not exist at the beginning of the 19th century. Hospitals in the early and middle 19th century were havens for the extremely poor and were considered a last resort. The hospital could provide only a few services, such as surgery. Modern concepts of hygiene and therapeutics were nonexistent. Ethnic and class prejudice virtually excluded many elements of society from even this rudimentary level of hospital care. In short, the hospital was widely viewed as a place best avoided. Someone who entered a hospital appeared unlikely to walk out.

In 1800, there were only two hospitals in the United States—Pennsylvania Hospital in Philadelphia, founded in 1752, and New York Hospital, founded in 1771. Although the number of hospitals gradually increased, they remained rare by modern standards until the end of the century. Even by 1873, the United States had fewer than 180 hospitals, with a total of less than 50,000 beds. This situation improved greatly after 1900, but most American

The operating room at the Polyclinic Medical School and Hospital, New York City, in 1901. Notice the insufficient concern for sterile conditions. Many surgeons failed to understand that infection was caused by matter introduced during an operation.

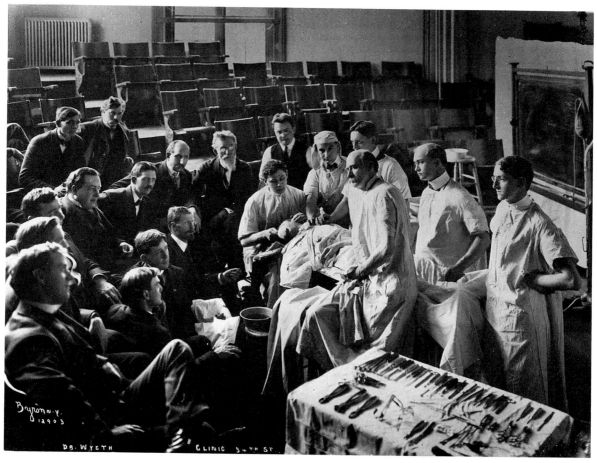

hospitals remained unsophisticated, ill-funded, poorly organized, and unspecialized in design almost until World War I. The result was an environment that could actually engender disease instead of curing it.

When an American fell ill during the early 19th century, hospital care, in most cases, was either unavailable or undesirable. Home care was prevalent. Practically any care that a hospital could deliver could be obtained outside the hospital as well. Moreover, physicians were not tied as closely to the hospital as they are today. Physicians could treat patients as effectively outside a hospital as within it. The doctor's instruments were portable, as was his diagnostic apparatus—his own eyes, ears, and brain.

In American cities during the early 19th century, the alternative to home care was the almshouse, which served as something approximating a hospital. The word *almshouse* has become a synonym for horror, with some reason. Almshouse care was devoted largely to criminals, orphans, and the very poor. Buildings were unspecialized and were not designed with sanitation, ventilation, or the logistics of patient care in mind. Contagious illnesses such as typhoid or diphtheria were dangers in the close quarters of the almshouse, and visitors to the wards might include rats and other vermin.

Early American hospitals treated many different illnesses, but major operations occurred there only rarely. Surgery as practiced in the early 19th century consisted largely of simple procedures such as setting broken bones. Comforts were few, because budgets were lean. Although hospitals prohibited some harmful activities, such as drinking and smoking, these prohibitions were due more to moral considerations than to medical concerns. (Gambling was also

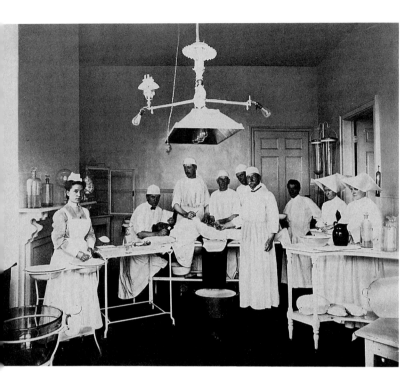

The operating room at a hospital in Mobile, Alabama, around 1900. Before anesthesia and antiseptics, surgery was brutal work. Speed was important—get in and out of the body as soon as possible. The range and volume of surgery, therefore, remained extremely limited as infection took a heavy toll on patients. Very rarely did the surgeon penetrate the major body cavities, and then only in desperation. By the 1890s and early 1900s, however, with major advances in medical science, particularly the development of X rays (1895), surgeons began to operate earlier and for a variety of conditions previously thought impossible.

banned.) Moral considerations might be disregarded, however, in the case of a paying patient.

Early hospitals were a microcosm of the social order of their time. Class distinctions did much to determine how well a patient was treated. A relatively affluent patient was likely to receive better care than a poor patient. Racial, religious, and cultural distinctions also influenced the quality of a patient's care. In Boston, for example, ethnic prejudice worked against the immigrant Irish.

The Civil War, which lasted from 1861 to 1865, brought about major changes in American hospital care, although many of those changes took a long time to be adopted by civilian hospitals. The need to care

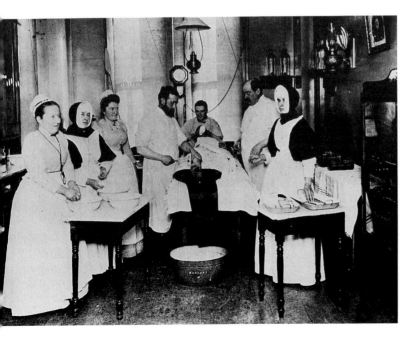

The operating room at St. Vincent's Hospital in Portland, Oregon, in 1885. The nuns in this photograph were members of the Sisters of Charity. This order received rigorous training in the care of the sick and became well known for its exceptional work in hospitals.

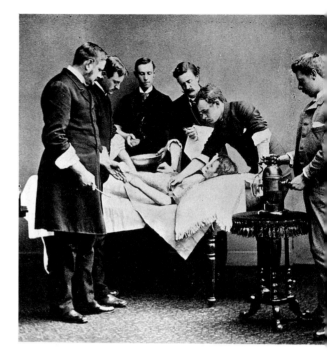

A rare 1870 photograph showing an antiseptic carbolic spray used during an operation. During the 1860s, the Scottish surgeon Joseph Lister observed that broken bones over which the skin remained intact usually healed without infection. Bones exposed to air, however, commonly developed pus infections. Lister concluded that particles in the air—what he called "disease dust"—were responsible. Lister sprayed a carbolic acid solution over patients in an attempt to prevent bacteria from growing in the wound.

for large numbers of wounded soldiers required numerous changes in health care and hospital design. The poorly organized, inadequately ventilated hospital of a generation earlier was no longer tolerable. In the war years, a new kind of hospital emerged. Larger and better organized than its predecessors, the wartime hospital reduced death rates and showed what redesign and reorganization might accomplish. These wartime facilities were disbanded, however, when hostilities ceased.

Following the war, the nation started considering how to extend hospital care to the entire range of society, including the very poor. The motive for this change was not purely moral. It had become apparent that improving medical care, through better hospitals for

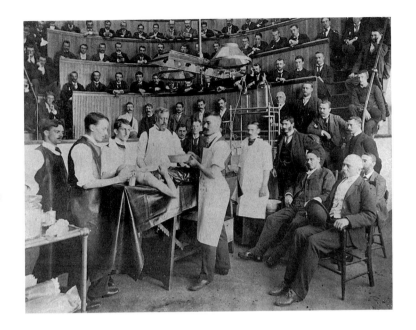

The operating room at Bellevue Hospital, New York City, 1898. Note the lack of masks, gloves, and surgical gowns.

the entire population, would confer great benefits on society as a whole. America was becoming a mature industrial society that required robust workers. A healthy worker was a better worker. Overall, a healthy population made better sense from an economic standpoint than a population where disease was allowed to spread either unchecked or poorly treated. Better health care required more and better hospitals.

The concept of adequate hospital care changed in many ways after the Civil War. Hospital functions had to expand beyond the rudimentary care of the early 19th century. No longer was it acceptable to concentrate on surgery alone. Hospitals also were expected to supply rest, decent food, and competent nursing care. Wartime hospital care had done much to provide such care and

29

The operating room of St. Joseph's Hospital, St. Paul, Minnesota, around 1890. The men in the background are medical students. Again, note the lack of masks and gloves.

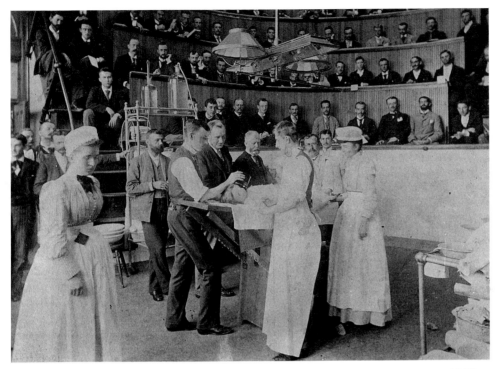

The photograph shows uniformed Bellevue nurses taking part in an operation in 1898.

support before the hospitals were disbanded at war's end. Now the nation had to build an infrastructure to replicate, and where possible improve upon, wartime hospital care for the benefit of the population as a whole.

By the mid-19th century, hospital care in the United States had improved vastly over that of Thomas Jefferson's day. Hygiene improved tremendously. Hospitals served better food, introduced more effective heating and ventilation, made floors easier to clean, and took advantage of new technologies such as electric lighting.

Diphtheria and typhoid became less of a threat. Statistics told the story. Once, admission to a hospital was seen as virtually a death sentence. In the first years after the Civil War, however, hospital death rates seldom rose above 10 percent. In other words, more than 9 out of every 10 patients who entered the hospital were discharged alive, if not totally cured.

Prejudice against hospitals remained, however, in part because of still-powerful class distinctions. Although hospitals of the mid-19th century existed largely to serve lower-class patients, a strong

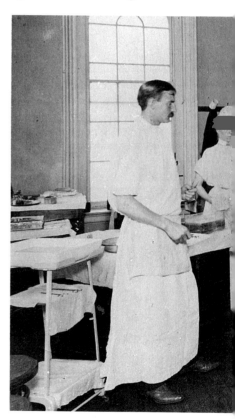

The operating room at St. Luke's Hospital, New York City, around 1890. The period from 1890 to 1900 was a time of unprecedented growth in the professionalization of American nursing. The experience of World War I (1914–18) definitely proved the superiority of the trained nurse over the untrained volunteer.

suspicion of and contempt for those same patients appears to have
guided hospital operations. The strong religious influence on hospital
care in the mid-19th century was also seen as oppressive in at least
some cases, because religious orders imposed strict discipline on
staff and patients alike. Then there were enduring ethnic prejudices,
which created resentment among the affected groups.

Despite great advances in hospital design and operation, hospital
care remained unavailable to much of the population. In the
1870s, there was one hospital bed for approximately every 2,000

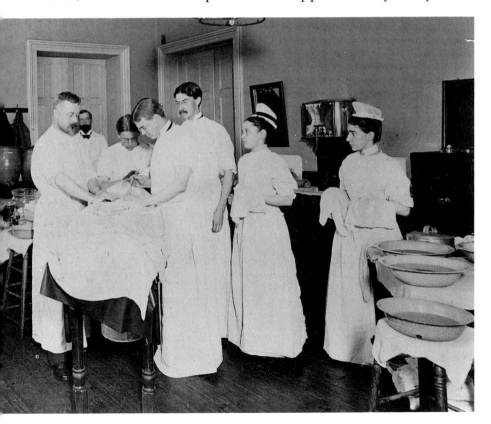

Improvements in the care of the sick after the Civil War corresponded with the development of an organized system to train nurses. In the 1870s, professional nursing schools began operating in the United States. The first was Bellevue Hospital Training School in New York City, founded in 1873. By 1920, there were almost 700 nursing schools, almost all under the control and direction of hospital authorities. The principal function of a nursing school was not formal education but service. Each hospital set its own standards for admission and graduation. When the Bellevue school opened, five students enrolled in the first class. The two-year program consisted almost entirely of practical work with only an occasional lecture. Students received $10 per month after a one-month probationary period. In 1874, the hospital adopted a standard nurse's uniform—the first in America—a long, blue seersucker dress with a white apron, collar and cuffs, and a white cap. A pin designed by Tiffany and Company in 1880 still distinguishes Bellevue graduates. Here are Bellevue Hospital nurses during laboratory instruction around 1900.

Americans, and hospital facilities were concentrated in a very few cities.

Nonetheless, the rise of the modern hospital had profound effects upon physicians' practices and careers. The hospital became the center of many physicians' activities. By the late 19th century, hospitals—which had scarcely existed in America only a generation earlier—had become essential to the practice of medicine and to doctors' careers. The hospital offered facilities, such as special wards for abdominal surgery, that could be found nowhere else. No longer was the American physician an independent practitioner, traveling

Volunteerism is an American tradition. This photograph, taken around 1905, shows an affluently dressed woman learning to make a hospital bed.

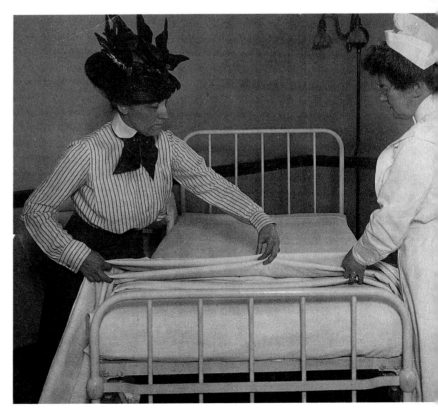

Dominique-Jean Larrey (1766–1842), a French surgeon, is credited with creating the ambulance during the Napoleonic Wars, where it was called the *hôpital ambulant,* the traveling hospital. These horse-drawn wagons were large enough to carry several stretchers. Larrey's vehicles went into operation as a military action started, boosting the morale of soldiers and affording a much greater opportunity for effective treatment. This photograph shows an ambulance belonging to New York City's Flower Hospital, around 1890.

rural roads to treat patients in their homes. The hospital-based practice was here to stay.

The doctor-hospital relationship, of course, worked two ways. Just as hospitals influenced doctors' practices, physicians exercised a strong influence on hospitals. Because professional physicians dominated American medicine by the latter half of the 19th century, they thought they had a right to exercise a large degree of control over hospitals. Doctors believed that the American hospital should satisfy their particular needs and interests above others. As a rule, this view had the support of trustees and the communities that

The Pan American Exposition opened in Buffalo, New York, on May 1, 1901. It celebrated technological progress made during the 19th century. On September 6, while visiting the exposition, President William McKinley was shot by an assassin. An ambulance (pictured right) took the wounded president to the exposition's emergency hospital. Though scarcely more than a first-aid station, it did have an operating room. No use was made of X rays to locate the bullet, although an X-ray machine was proudly displayed at the fair. The wound was stitched without removing the bullet, and blood poisoning developed. The president died on September 14.

supported the hospitals. It was also a narrow view of a hospital's purpose, however, and was sometimes difficult to reconcile with alternative views that put the patients' interests first.

Major changes came to nursing as well as to doctors' practices during the rise of hospitals. In the mid-19th century, nursing was unspecialized. It was not yet distinct from domestic service. In other words, there was not much difference between a nurse and a maid. The famous nurse Florence Nightingale essentially founded modern nursing by creating a more highly trained nursing corps. As a result, hospitals of the late 19th century could draw upon a pool of specially trained, disciplined nurses.

A revolution in transportation and communication helped support the hospitals and hospital-centered medical practice. As automobiles came into widespread use, patients could come to the hospital, where the doctor would be waiting for them. The telephone helped too, by allowing doctors to schedule appointments at the hospital and thus make more efficient use of time.

As hospitals grew bigger and more sophisticated, however, medical care began to lose a certain human touch. Hospitals became more impersonal and bureaucratic. This change occurred in the interest of efficiency. Trustees and administrators aimed to establish routines, simplify procedures, keep errors to a minimum, and cut costs. Such goals sometimes required ruthless measures. Those measures may have helped make better use of hospital resources but also contributed to a perception that hospitals were cold places where the patient was treated as a unit to be numbered, processed, and then discharged as soon as possible.

In the early 1900s, hospitals changed their focus to emphasize health care for the middle class. This change reflected the

By the 1880s, the medical profession recognized that good nursing played an important part in a patient's treatment as well as in preventive medicine. The popular image of a nurse as a woman who was "too old, too weak, too drunken, too dirty, too stolid, or too bad to do anything else"—in the sarcastic words of Florence Nightingale—was being overturned by the trained, skilled, and competent nurses emerging from the new teaching hospitals. New York City's Infant Welfare Society had a visiting nurse program to care for slum children. This engraving shows the anatomical lecture room of the Medical College for Women in New York City.

transformation in American society, as trade and industry created a substantial middle class in urban areas served by hospitals.

In only a century, the American hospital grew and developed from virtually nothing at all into a mighty institution that dominated medicine. By 1910, the United States had more than 4,000 hospitals with some 421,000 beds. (These figures do not include mental hospitals and hospitals for treating chronic diseases such as tuberculosis.) In 1820, hospitals were essentially nonexistent. A hundred years later, medical care could not exist without them. Hospitals dominated medical education. They were the preferred place to practice medicine. They had replaced the home and family as providers of medical care. Hospitals offered care to poor and well-off alike. They had become places of hope rather than symbols of despair. By the second decade of the 20th century, much of the population was born in a hospital, received treatment in a hospital for serious illnesses, and eventually died in a hospital.

But the hospital system had serious problems. These included the depersonalization of health care, as well as what some observers saw as an overemphasis on treating acute illnesses and on the particular needs and priorities of physicians.

PHYSICIANS AND
THE SOCIAL STRUCTURE

THE PHYSICIAN TODAY IS AN INFLUENTIAL FIGURE IN THE community, and the doctor's profession as a whole is known for its wealth, political power, and domination of the health care industry. For decades, the title "doctor" has been synonymous with prosperity, and the expression "doctor's orders" has symbolized obedience to authority.

A hundred years ago, however, the American physician was in a much less commanding position. Doctors then were relatively poor and low in social standing. Moreover, they were virtually powerless to set and enforce standards for practice and medical education and were beset by internal feuds that sometimes came close to physical violence.

The medical profession overcame these problems through a combination of diplomacy, compromise, and "federalization," which healed the major divisions within the profession and ultimately gave doctors a formidable power structure comparable in some ways to the United States government itself.

In June 1859, the Swiss banker J. Henri Dunant witnessed the horrors of a battle between France and Austria. There were only two physicians to care for some 6,000 men. Subsequently, Dunant appealed to European governments to establish an international organization to provide volunteer nursing aid on battlefields. This was the beginning of the Red Cross. This painting shows the signing by 12 nations, on August 22, 1864, of the Geneva Convention, a set of principles protecting those wounded in war, the supplies needed for their care, and the volunteers assisting them. Each government pledged to consider the Red Cross nurses noncombatants and to respect their facilities. In 1882, through the efforts of Clara Barton, the United States Congress ratified the Treaty of Geneva.

At the same time, the public's view of medicine and the medical profession changed in ways that helped increase and consolidate the authority of physicians and made the average American more dependent on doctors' judgments and services. The economic environment of the United States also changed so as to make medical care affordable to large numbers of people and thus enhance the income, social standing, and authority of doctors all at once.

The problems of physicians in 19th-century America stemmed largely from public perceptions of them. The people simply did not hold doctors in high esteem. This attitude stemmed partly from the democratic nature of American society. The public was suspicious of elites, whether political or professional. Such suspicion discouraged the formation of a powerful, authoritative medical profession.

Also, the hub of modern medical treatment—the hospital—had not developed yet. In the early and middle 19th century, as in the century before, much medical care was conducted at home. Popular medical manuals for home use downplayed the value of professional physicians and their skills. There was a reason for this attitude, beyond the democratic, antielitist views of the American people. Professional doctors existed, but their training and knowledge were not of uniform quality. Almost anyone of certain means could set himself up as a physician. It is only a slight exaggeration to say that no special qualifications were needed to practice medicine. It was not even necessary to devote one's whole career to medicine. An ordinary tradesman might practice medicine on the side. This situation did little to encourage widespread trust of doctors.

Physicians also had competition from "lay healers." These included herbalists who used botanical remedies to treat illness. Native American lay healers known as "Indian doctors" also were active and enjoyed a high reputation. Then there were "bonesetters" skilled in treating fractured and dislocated limbs. Competition from such nonprofessionals restricted the authority and influence of professional physicians.

Competition also was intense among professional physicians themselves. On the individual level, doctors often tried to weaken one another's practices by stealing patients. Disagreements on medical theory and therapies divided the profession even further. For example, the Thomsonians, followers of an untrained New England "doctor" named Samuel Thomson, believed that cold temperatures caused all disease and that applying heat—through hot baths or spicy foods—could cure it.

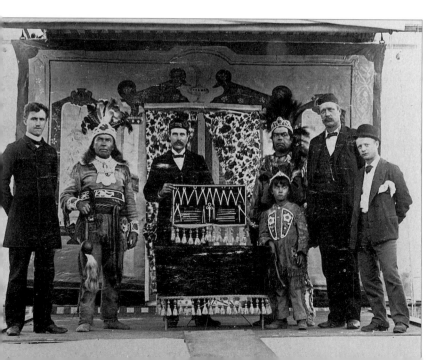

The famous Kickapoo Medicine Company show, in Marine, Minnesota, around 1890.

Edward Terry (1844–1912) was England's leading comedian. His eccentric acting and singing created a style that had many imitators. This sheet music was written by Francis C. Burhand, a well-known humorist, for Terry's mid-1870 hit comedy *Camaralzaman*. Here, Terry is parodying a patent medicine salesman.

Another group, the homeopaths, thought that one could cure disease by administering a drug that caused similar symptoms when given to a healthy person. "Like cures like" was the homeopathic motto. The homeopaths also believed that drugs worked best when greatly diluted in water. The famous French cartoonist Honoré Daumier once drew a mocking portrait of two would-be homeopaths

45

formulating their philosophy: take a small grain of "nothing," dissolve it in water, dilute the solution millions of times, and remember the most important step—pay for the prescription!

Yet another group, the eclectics, believed in a little of everything. They accepted much of conventional medicine but also subscribed to herbal therapy. In some ways, the eclectics were ahead of their time. They opposed, for example, the harmful practice of bleeding, or drawing off blood from a patient in large amounts.

Infant incubators are used to provide a warm environment for babies born prematurely. This device dates from 1890.

Aspirin, a derivative of salicylic acid, has been known since 1853. The process for mass-producing aspirin was developed by Bayer, a German corporation, in 1893. Because of its safety and usefulness in relieving pain and fever, aspirin quickly became the world's most widely used medication. Also advertised here is a heroin product produced by Bayer Pharmaceutical Products around 1900. Synthesized in 1874, by 1898 heroin was considered the ideal nonaddictive substitute for morphine and codeine.

An 1868 advertisement promising $1,000 if Orton's Preparation does not stop the tobacco habit.

These various groups had their own medical schools and struggled against one another for decades. Eventually, however, they made peace after a fashion and could then concentrate on improving standards for medical education and practice—notably the licensing of physicians.

Imposing minimum standards on medical education was difficult. The medical schools wanted to make money as well as train doctors. Higher standards, however, meant fewer students and lower revenues. The schools therefore had reason to oppose improved standards, and did so. Fears of diminished enrollment and consequent bankruptcy, however, turned out to be groundless. After Harvard University upgraded its medical curriculum in the 1870s, enrollment actually increased.

Effective medical licensing was attained only after long effort on both the state and national levels. The U.S. Supreme Court approved state licensing of physicians in 1888. A doctor claimed that he had been convicted and fined unjustly under an 1882 West Virginia law that required a doctor to have a degree from a reputable medical school. The Supreme Court ruled against the doctor and said plainly that states could require licensing of physicians and could deny the right to practice to a physician without a license.

Another major event in the history of 19th-century American medicine was the formation of what would become the American Medical Association (AMA) in 1846. The AMA's goals included higher standards for medical education and practice. Its early years were stormy, because the medical profession in America included so many feuding groups and because opposition to reform was strong. By the early 20th century, however, the AMA became the embodiment of mainstream medical practice.

48

(continued on page 53)

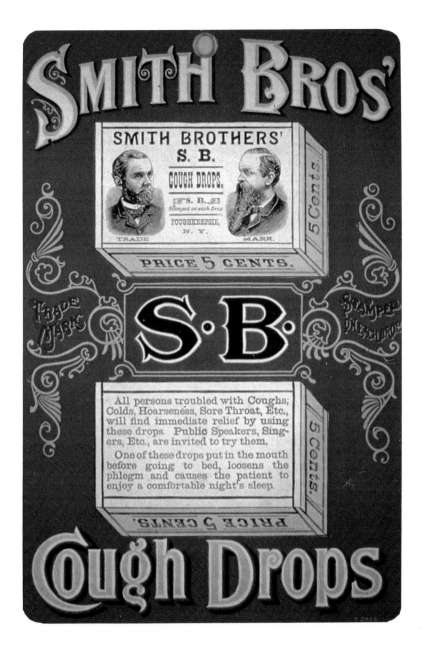

An early advertisement for the Smith Brothers' famous cough drops.

The Kickapoo Medicine Company, founded by John Healy and Charles Bigelow in 1881, remained a successful business for more than 30 years. It employed Indian performers to stage colorful shows during which patent medicines of roots, barks, gums, oils, berries, herbs—and alcohol—were sold. The two men created the memorable Chief Sagwa and the legendary Kickapoo tribe, a name few could forget. The original Sagwa tonic was made from aloe and stale beer. Several hundred Indian shows toured America, often staying in cities three weeks at a time. In winter, they performed in town halls. In warmer months, the shows took place under large tents in a carnival atmosphere. Hired Indians wore war dress and carried tomahawks and knives. These popular shows were booked several years in advance. Several toured Europe and attracted capacity crowds awed by real Indians and their medical cures. Healy and Bigelow became millionaires. The usual sales routine included five Indians who merely grunted, but the sixth would deliver an impassioned talk in his "native" language. His "faithful scout" translated the dramatic tale that described the

mysterious origins of the tonics that had saved countless lives of fearless braves. By 1900, Kickapoo Cough Syrup had become the most widely used remedy in America. Its main ingredient was rum, and it promised "a quick cure" for any cough. Al Capp, creator of the popular *Li'l Abner* comic strip, immortalized "kickapoo juice."

Sarsaparilla was used in medicines for centuries. By 1900, tonics containing this root became popular cures, promising to "eliminate poisons from blood and tissues" while "purifying the system." Sarsaparilla tonics contained a generous amount of alcohol. The Ayer's brand apparently contained the most alcohol. It was said that a bottle of Ayer's would not freeze in Maine's coldest winters.

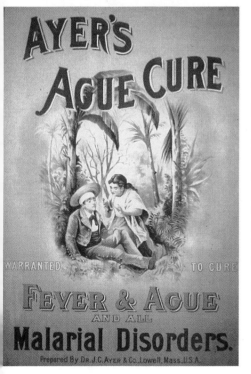

Dr. James Ayer's remedies dominated the patent medicine field 100 years ago. Ague—fever and chills accompanied by pains in the joints—is called the flu today. Ayer promoted "family remedies." They included a hair restorer, an extract of sarsaparilla, and a cherry pectoral. With each new product, Ayer doubled his advertising budget. He distributed a patent medicine almanac—"second only to the Bible in circulation," proclaimed its cover. Money rolled in, and by 1870 Ayer had become one of the wealthiest men in Massachusetts.

51

Lydia E. Pinkham (1819–1893) claimed that her Vegetable Compound cured every "female complaint." What started in 1875 as a home remedy for her Lynn, Massachusetts, neighbor rapidly became a spectacularly successful business. Like other patent medicines, the label and trademark were registered with the United States Patent Office, but the ingredients remained secret. The compound, a mixture of ground herbs and roots, contained 15 percent alcohol, added, the label explained, "solely as a solvent and preservative." One tablespoon was recommended every four hours. By 1881, sales exceeded 200,000 bottles a year. Mrs. Pinkham and her sons energetically promoted the product through extensive advertising—spending $1 million a year by 1914. The Pinkhams capitalized on women's dissatisfaction with male doctors' treatment of gynecological illnesses. They invited women to write for "honest, expert advice, free of charge." Supposedly Mrs.

Pinkham—and later an all-female staff—promptly responded to hundreds of letters a day. "Men *never* see your letters." "No Boys Around," began one ad. "All letters are received, opened, read, and answered by women only." Sales boomed. During the 1920s, the federal government forced the Pinkham Medicine Company to reduce their claims—and the alcohol content. Nevertheless, Pinkham's remedies had a solid following among older women who felt they were using an herbal cure similar to those brewed by their mothers and grandmothers. In 1968, the company, faced with shrinking sales, sold their assets.

(continued from page 48)

The AMA consolidated its power by adopting a federal structure much like that of the U.S. government. This structure incorporated medical societies on local, state, and national levels. The result was an organization that could represent its members' interests effectively on a national basis. What we know as the medical establishment had appeared.

At the same time, the public's view of the medical profession was undergoing a dramatic change. Medical reform—specifically, better education and licensing—improved the collective reputation of physicians. The public put greater faith in medical advice and in doctors' authority. Public trust in and dependence on physicians increased. Now the doctor was widely respected, if not actually revered. Financial success became easier for physicians too, as the increasing affluence of American society combined with increasing public trust made doctors' work more lucrative.

American medicine in the 19th century was a male-dominated profession. Although women commonly served as healers early in the century, the doctor's profession was largely closed to them. Women who tried to enter medical school faced ridicule, ostracism, and sometimes bodily assault. Nonetheless, women kept trying to enter the medical fraternity because they thought they had a unique contribution to make. Women believed they could help to humanize a profession often characterized by its cold and insensitive attitude toward the patient.

Critics of medical education for women argued that training for the medical profession would encourage women to disregard their responsibilities for rearing children. According to another such argument, formal medical training would harden women and should be disallowed. Skeptics said there were too many physicians already,

Advertising for popular home remedies appealed to fears of medical treatment and surgery. In 1876, the Lydia E. Pinkham Company introduced its vegetable compound for "female weaknesses." Women were urged to write Mrs. Pinkham about their complaints, a practice continued after Lydia Pinkham died in 1893. Through its extensive promotional efforts, the company appealed to Victorian modesty to draw women away from doctors. "Do you want a strange man to hear about your diseases?" asked one advertisement. The Pinkham Company offered $5,000 "deposited with the National Bank of Lynn, Mass." to anyone who could show that testimonial letters were false or "published before obtaining the writer's special permission."

A CRY FOR HELP

Result of a Prompt Reply

Two Open Letters that Should Prompt Thousands of American Women to Go and Do Likewise

LITTLE FALLS, Minn., May 11, 1894.
"I am suffering, and need your aid. I have terrible pains in both sides, extending down to the front of my limbs and lower part of my back, attended by backache and pains in the back of the neck and ears. The doctors have given me opiates to quiet the pain. I have a very high fever nearly all the time. I am nervous and cannot stand. My doctor says I must keep in bed. Now I place myself under your care. I am only twenty-one years old and too young to suffer so much."
MRS. CHARLES PARKER.

The above letter from Mrs. Parker was received by Mrs. Pinkham at Lynn, Mass., May 15, and received a prompt reply. The following letter reached Mrs. Pinkham five months later. Note the result:

LITTLE FALLS, Minn., Sept. 21.
"I deem it my duty to announce the fact to my fellow sufferers of all female complaints that **Lydia E. Pinkham's** treatment and Vegetable Compound have entirely cured me of all the pains and suffering I was enduring when I wrote her last May. I followed her advice to the letter, and the result is simply wonderful. May Heaven bless her and the good work she is doing for our sex! If you are sick or in trouble write to Mrs. Pinkham. Her advice invariably brings relief. Your letter will be received, read and answered by one of our own sex."
MRS. CHARLES PARKER.

Druggists say there is a tremendous demand for **Lydia E. Pinkham's** Vegetable Compound; and it is doing lots of good, that is the blessed thing about it.

Three Books Worth Getting—"Guide to Health." "Woman's Beauty, Peril, Duty." "Woman's Triumph."—These are FREE

Lydia E. Pinkham Medicine Co., Lynn, Mass.

GORDAK'S
HIGHLY APPROVED
OPODELDOC,
AN INESTIMABLE REMEDY FOR THE
RHEUMATISM.

For pain in the Side, Back and Limbs; it speedily cures violent Bruises; valuable in Swellings; it will remove Humours and Pimples; most efficacious for Chilblains and Stiffness in the Joints; and is also a most excellent Salve for Sores, and is well known to heal the hardest wound in forty-eight hours.

DIRECTIONS.

In cases of the Rheumatism, pains in the Side, Back and Limbs, Bruises, Swellings, Chilblains, and Stiffness in the Joints, one large tea-spoonful at the time will be sufficient, to be well rubbed on the part affected, before a fire, three or four times a day. In Humours or Pimples a very small quantity at the time will be sufficient, to apply every three hours to the part affected. In Sores and Wounds use it for a Salve.

Price 33 1-3 Cents per Bottle.

None are genuine unless stamped on the Cork and signed on the Label

JOHN MARSH, No. 84, Washington Street, and WM. C. STIMPSON & CO. south side of Faneuil Hall, Boston, General Sole Agents for the only Inventor and Proprietor.

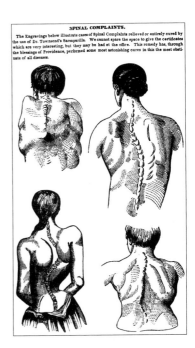

SPINAL COMPLAINTS.

The Engravings below illustrate cases of Spinal Complaints relieved or entirely cured by the use of Dr. Townsend's Sarsaparilla. We cannot spare the space to give the certificates which are very interesting, but they may be had at the office. This remedy has, through the blessings of Providence, performed some most astonishing cures in this the most obstinate of all diseases.

Medical history abounds with quack cures. The objective was to make money by deceiving a public eager for successful treatments. In 1906, Congress enacted a Pure Food and Drug Act. This law was the first to attack fraudulent medical advertising. While it did not ensure full protection for consumers, it curbed some of the worst abuses.

55

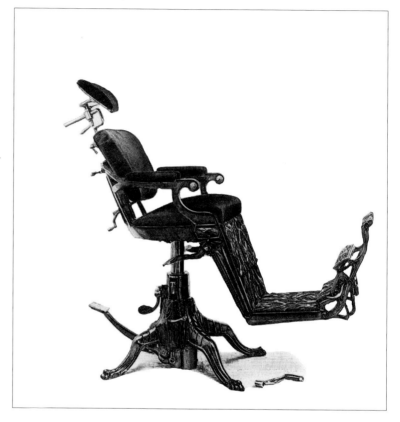

An advertisement for a "pedal-lever dental chair" from an 1877 *Catalogue of Dental Materials*.

and therefore women would add to the glut of doctors. Also, many male physicians simply felt threatened by the entry of women into a formerly all-male preserve. Only about one-third of regular medical schools in the 1890s allowed women to enter.

Barriers to women entering medicine were so formidable in the 19th century that many American women went for training in Europe, where opposition was less pronounced. Women also founded their own medical schools in America. At first, critics

A hand-operated eyeball vibrator, designed to ease eye strain, sold around the turn of the century.

expressed concern that these schools would not provide adequate training. These schools, however, followed high standards that made such criticism invalid.

Despite opposition from men, women entered medical school and became doctors. Their training was not restricted to schools for women. The Johns Hopkins Medical School in Baltimore, for example, opened in 1892 and admitted women on the same basis as men. Nonetheless, opposition remained.

57

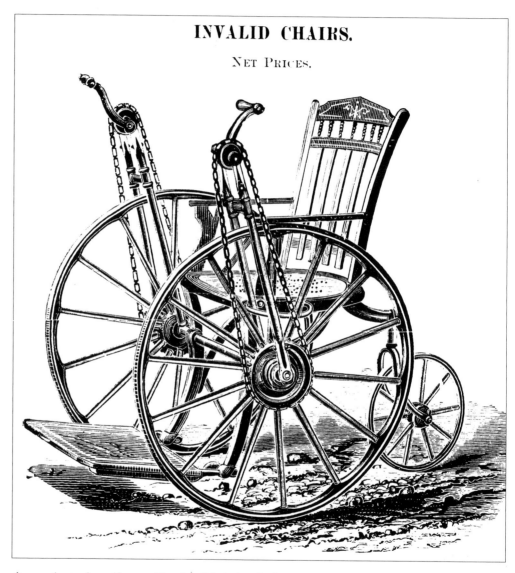

INVALID CHAIRS.

Net Prices.

A woodcut of a self-propelling invalid chair, which was patented in 1880.

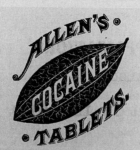

For Colds, Sore Throat, Nervousness, Neuralgia, Headache, Sleeplessness, Dyspepsia, Indigestion, Heartburn, and Flatulency.

USED BY ELOCUTIONISTS, VOCALISTS, AND ACTORS.

NASAL TABLOIDS.

For Catarrh, Asthma, Hay Fever, Cold in the Head.

COCAINE OINTMENT.

For Burns, Scalds, Sunburn, Prickly Heat, Eczema, Hives, Itching Skin Eruptions, Mosquito Bites.

PRICE LIST.

TABLETS,	$4.00 PER DOZEN.
OINTMENT,	4.00 " "
NASAL TABLOIDS,	8.00 " "

For Sale by Wholesale Druggists and

ALLEN COCAINE MFG. CO.,

1254 BROADWAY, NEW YORK.

By the 1880s, cocaine was widely used as an anesthetic. In 1898, cocaine became the first drug injected into the spinal canal to produce anesthesia. Once its dangers were realized, however, other less toxic and nonaddictive agents were developed.

Difficulties also faced the female practitioner after graduation. Setting up a private practice was difficult. Male physicians opposed female doctors. Women patients, however, sought out female physicians and thus helped keep female doctors in business. Women in medicine also found opportunities in institutions such as asylums and "water cure" establishments, known today as spas.

Women also started their own hospitals and dispensaries, as they had set up their own medical schools. These institutions included the New York Infirmary in Manhattan and the Children's Hospital in San Francisco. Yet there were limits to what women could do on their own, and even as the modern hospital emerged, with its unprecedented opportunities for teaching, learning, and successful practice, women in 19th-century America continued to have trouble obtaining appointments on hospital staffs.

In a hundred years, the social standing of physicians in America changed greatly. The medical profession in the early 19th century was humble, disorganized, and held almost in contempt. By 1900, it was largely unified and had its own national organization to promote its interests. Medical reform had increased the respectability, professionalism, and social authority of doctors. There was now a medical establishment—something that would have been a meaningless concept at the beginning of the century.

THE PROBLEMS
OF PUBLIC HEALTH

PORTRAITS OF WOMEN FAMED FOR THEIR BEAUTY IN THE late 18th and early 19th centuries may look plain to modern eyes. That is because their era had a standard of beauty very different from ours today. In George Washington's time, a beautiful woman was one whose skin had not been pitted and ravaged by smallpox. Her nose might be long, and her chin might be weak, but smooth skin made her gorgeous. That bit of cultural history gives us a glimpse of what life in 19th-century America was like before modern public health measures reduced the potential for epidemics.

Just as it is difficult for Americans in our own time to imagine the conditions in Civil War field hospitals, so it is hard now to comprehend how many devastating diseases, kept in check today by public health controls, swept through American cities in the 19th century. Cholera, typhoid, and diphtheria were only three of the major killers in 19th-century America. As a rule, contemporary lithographs of prosperous American cities and happy households do not depict the then ever-present danger of epidemic disease, which could strike virtually anywhere, with effects as dreadful as those of an invading army.

The threat from epidemic illness was due largely to poor sanitation and to disease-carrying insects such as flies. The modern arrangement of indoor plumbing tied to an extensive municipal sewer system did not exist. The outhouse was a familiar fixture of American cities. Large quantities of human waste sat exposed to the air, so that flies could carry the waste—and its load of disease-causing microbes—virtually anywhere, in an era before the widespread use of window screens. The famed journalist H. L. Mencken, in a memoir of his childhood in 19th-century Baltimore, recalled how his mother waged war against swarms of flies in their home during the summer, all the while giving thanks that Baltimore was not as pestilential as nearby Washington!

Overcoming such threats to public health required vast effort and expense. It also required both state and federal governments to rethink their roles and responsibilities. Charged with promoting the general welfare and providing for the common defense, the government came to recognize that the former required a healthy population and the latter included defense against contagious disease as well as enemy bullets.

Voluntary organizations such as the American Public Health Association (APHA), which originated in 1872, gave public health measures and preventive medicine an early boost. These associations supported the nursing profession by supplying trained nurses to the sick and the poor in their homes. One such organization was the New York City Mission, started in 1877. Other cities, including Philadelphia and Buffalo, followed New York City's lead in the 1880s.

Vaccinating the baby, from an 1870 print. In 1800, there were approximately 4,000 physicians in the United States. Fewer than 500 held university degrees; the rest had learned through apprenticeships. That year, Dr. Benjamin Waterhouse introduced vaccination to America. This eventually led to the control of smallpox, an acute and highly contagious disease which leaves permanent scars on the skin. Previously, more than 50 major smallpox epidemics had scourged North America. During the last year of the French and Indian War (1763), smallpox was used as a biological weapon when Lord Jeffrey Amherst ordered blankets infected with smallpox distributed among Indian tribes supporting the French. Vaccination, successfully demonstrated by the English physician Edward Jenner, consisted of rubbing cowpox virus into the skin. This produced antibodies against smallpox. Doctors vaccinated when they could, but religious beliefs, superstitions, public ignorance, and fear prevented mandatory vaccinations in most states until the 1950s.

By 1920, about 4,000 organizations were involved in public health nursing and employed some 11,000 nurses.

Public health improvement, however, did not remain a purely voluntary effort for long. In a pattern familiar to 19th-century America, states moved in quickly where the voluntary groups had shown the way. In response to an APHA campaign, states moved to establish their own official boards of health. The APHA's influence also extended to the national level. In 1878, for example, the APHA set up a committee to draft legislation that was passed in 1879 as the National Public Health Law.

The formation of state boards of health did much to make effective public health measures possible. For example, state health boards supported bacteriological laboratories that monitored food and water for disease-causing agents. The state boards also handled such diverse duties as compiling vital statistics and preventing and controlling communicable diseases. There were many cases when public health measures, to be effective, required the state's authority. Once state health boards appeared, interstate cooperation became possible; before long, the federal government's role in public health care increased as well.

Today the federal government is deeply involved in public health. This was not the case in the nation's early years. The federal government did little to protect public health in the late 18th and early 19th centuries, partly because there was little the government could do. The federal budget was minuscule by modern standards, and the needed medical knowledge and infrastructure had not yet appeared.

The federal government's role in public health began in a small way in 1798, when the Marine Hospital Service was established. The service operated hospitals in Norfolk, Virginia, Boston, Massachusetts, and other cities. Its effectiveness was limited, however, because of poor administration. Not until 1870 was the service reorganized on the model of the United States Army Medical Department. The reorganization represented a vast improvement, but the service had problems dealing with state laws.

In 1902, the service became the Public Health and Marine Hospital Service and established a Hygienic Laboratory to regulate interstate sales of serums, toxins, and related products. Ten years later, in 1912, the service became the United States Public Health Service. It had the

64

(continued on page 69)

Tonics, liniments, and painkillers contained herbal ingredients, such as anise and coriander and vegetable bitters, the most popular being cinchona and gentian. By 1900, virtually every botanical combination appeared in thousands of patent medicines. Most common mixtures included cloves, cinnamon, rhubarb, and orange peel—mixed with a generous amount of alcohol.

Today, the federal Food and Drug Administration prohibits the sale of medicines with secret ingredients. All medicines must be clearly labeled as to contents and any special restriction on usage. Until the mid-1920s, however, it was possible to patent remedies that contained secret compounds. These patent medicines were sold "over the counter"—directly to the customer without a physician's prescription. Most patent medicines promised miraculous cures or the customer's money would be refunded. Since an overwhelming majority of Americans 100 years ago never saw a medical doctor or a dentist, these colorfully advertised remedies became a major business.

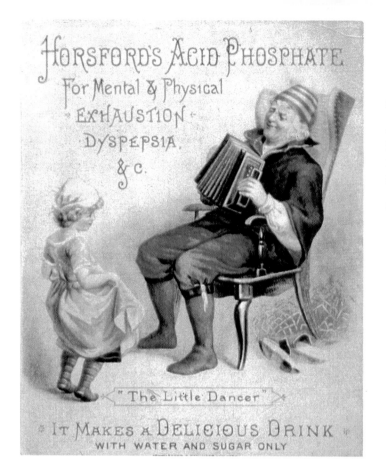

HORSFORD'S ACID PHOSPHATE
For Mental & Physical
EXHAUSTION
DYSPEPSIA
&c.

"The Little Dancer"

IT MAKES A DELICIOUS DRINK
WITH WATER AND SUGAR ONLY

An 1890 advertising card promoting a popular fruit-flavored phosphoric powder to cure dyspepia, or indigestion. When mixed with water and sugar, it made "a delicious drink."

Dozens of liniments promised a cure for rheumatism, frostbite, cramps, bronchitis, and muscle spasms. These patent medicines were sold by mail and by druggists. Large cardboard signs and colorful window displays promoted the medicines. In many states, especially the Deep South and rural New England, the drinking of liquor violated the law. These tonics, which contained as much as 40 percent alcohol, evaded prohibition.

DR. MORSE'S COMPOUND SYRUP OF
YELLOW DOCK ROOT,
Is the best Blood Purifier Ever Prepared. Cures all Humors, Dyspepsia, Biliousness, Constipation, Dizziness, Headache, Liver and Kidney Diseases, and General Debility.
—PREPARED BY THE—
MORSE YELLOW DOCK ROOT SYRUP CO.
PROVIDENCE, R. I.

By 1900, dozens of cough medicines lined the shelves of local drugstores. "Celebrated" physicians endorsed these products with promises that only "pure" ingredients were used. "We guarantee all that we claim" became the most commonly used phrase on labels.

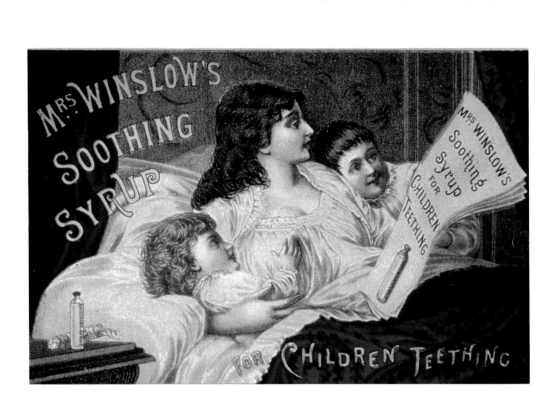

The image of a well-gowned and well-groomed mother with her children conveys dignity in this colorful Victorian-era advertisement. By the 1890s, patent medicines had become a most profitable and competitive business.

Tonics promised cures for virtually every pain and muscle spasm. These products were promoted through picturesque cards, posters, and displays.

(continued from page 64)

authority to distribute federal assistance to state and local health departments. The Public Health Service also handled interstate control of sanitation and measures to control communicable diseases.

Two developments combined to make public health measures increasingly effective in America during the late 19th century. One trend, as noted earlier, was the establishment of voluntary groups and government agencies to provide needed resources and coordinate required services. The second trend was a clearer understanding of the nature and origins of epidemic disease.

Progress in the war against epidemics was slow until their bacterial origin was established in the late 19th century. Before it was known that bacteria were responsible for many epidemic diseases, there simply was no way to initiate appropriate public health measures. Much of the credit for determining that bacteria cause disease goes to the French chemist Louis Pasteur, who proved that a microbe caused anthrax, a deadly disease of sheep and humans. German bacteriologist Robert Koch also helped to expand knowledge of epidemic disease by tracing its origin to microbes.

Despite the work of Koch, Pasteur, and other pioneer microbiologists, American physicians were reluctant at first to accept the microbial theory of disease. One alternative theory of that time was that miasmas, mysterious vapors thought to have disease-causing properties, were responsible for spreading illness. Nonetheless, America finally came around to the microbial theory, and by the late 19th century was making dramatic advances in public health protection.

In 1887, the United States became the first nation to set up a bacteriological laboratory for public health purposes, at the Staten Island Marine Hospital in New York. The laboratory analyzed

Asiatic cholera was never more than a potential danger in America in the decades following the Civil War; yet it received enormous attention from newspapers in all sections of the country. This acute, infectious, often-fatal disease, endemic to China and India, periodically broke out in epidemic proportions in areas with the poorest sanitary conditions. Most major urban hygienic campaigns in the 1880s were sparked by a perceived imminent danger of an outbreak of cholera. As with yellow fever, cholera created panic. As the disease spread into Europe in the late 1870s, fear gripped American cities. Responding to demands from newspapers and civic groups, the New York City Department of Health began a major campaign to end the worst sanitary conditions within the city.

FRANK LESLIE'S ILLUSTRAT WEEKLY

Vol. LXXV.—No. 1933.
ht, 1892, by ARKELL WEEKLY CO.
All Rights Reserved.

NEW YORK, SEPTEMBER 29, 1892.

The association of rats with the spread of disease, especially bubonic plague, has been known since ancient times. This 1890 photograph shows a municipal exterminator service.

samples of food and water. Five years later, in 1892, the New York City Bacteriological Laboratory was established. This laboratory conducted a famous study of a typhoid outbreak in Plymouth, Pennsylvania, and helped to save New York City from an epidemic of cholera in 1892. Soon, other cities set up their own bacteriological laboratories for public health protection. The laboratories had many other duties besides monitoring foodstuffs and water for dangerous microbes. They also distributed vaccines and antitoxins to doctors and public health offices. State health boards supported the laboratories.

The Civil War, almost half a century earlier, marked the boundary between the old era of American medicine and the new. The Spanish-American War, at the century's end, showed how far medicine, and public health medicine in particular, had advanced in that time. Disease was still a major killer in the army during the 1890s. About one-fifth of the troops camped in the United States during the Spanish-American war contracted typhoid, and illness is thought to have killed more than 10 times as many troops as combat did. In the Civil War, this problem would have been all but insoluble. By the 1890s, however, public health authorities had the knowledge and authority to attack typhoid and win.

Bacteriological studies had shown that a particular bacillus caused typhoid. It was also known that contaminated drinking water spread the disease. That knowledge put the conquest of typhoid within reach. In 1898, the U.S. Army set up a commission to study the typhoid problem. The commission included Major

By the 1880s, tuberculosis had become the leading cause of death in American cities. It was realized, however, that the disease was communicable, preventable, and curable. Supervision and isolation of those infected could lead to a restoration of health. This ferryboat, one of many, was used around 1910 as a "floating hospital" to give tuberculosis patients fresh air and clean surroundings.

American cities of the 1870s and 1880s had an excess of sweatshop factories where workers labored 12 hours a day. But nothing compared with the hazards of tobacco in "home factories." Here, for meager wages, women and children endured the most sickening smell as they stripped tobacco leaves. *Harper's Magazine* described the effects of endless hours of this work: "Their eyes are dead, a stupor overcomes them, their nerves are unsettled and their lungs diseased in almost every case."

In American cities of the 1860s through the 1880s, garbage pickup services virtually did not exist. New York's sidewalks were piled high with the wastes of daily life, including kitchen slops, cinders, coal dust, horse manure, broken cobblestones, and dumped merchandise. There was hardly a street in lower Manhattan that a pedestrian could negotiate without climbing over a heap of trash or, in rain, wading through a bed of slime. This engraving shows raw garbage being loaded on a barge in New York City in 1860, with the poorest of the poor picking through the refuse looking for anything still useful.

Returning medieval crusaders introduced many contagious diseases into Europe. The most notorious was the Black Death, or bubonic plague. During the 14th century, perhaps one-quarter of Europe's population succumbed to this highly infectious disease, which caused death within a few days, often within hours. In Venice, for example, because of fear of the plague, all immigrants were required to be isolated for 40 days, giving us the term *quarantine,* from *quaranta,* Italian for "forty." Improved sanitary measures, however, brought the plague under control by the mid-19th century. Here, public health inspectors are examining rats suspected of carrying bubonic plague in 1914. Ships arriving in the United States were routinely checked for infected rodents.

During most of the 19th century, the poor and immigrant sick were sent to publicly supported almshouses, or "poor houses." Often squalid and overcrowded, they gave a minimal level of medical treatment—a symbol to many that the poor must not become dependent on government assistance. Social reformers in the 1870s and 1880s attempted to remove orphaned children, the insane, the blind, and the very sick from these almshouses and place them in voluntary hospitals—that is, voluntary because they were financed by donations rather than by taxes. Ethnic and religious differences between physicians and patients also widened the social distance that separated them. More than 70 percent of those treated in New York City almshouses during the 1860s were Irish laborers. This 1860 engraving shows conditions in New York's Bellevue Hospital, formerly the New York Almshouse.

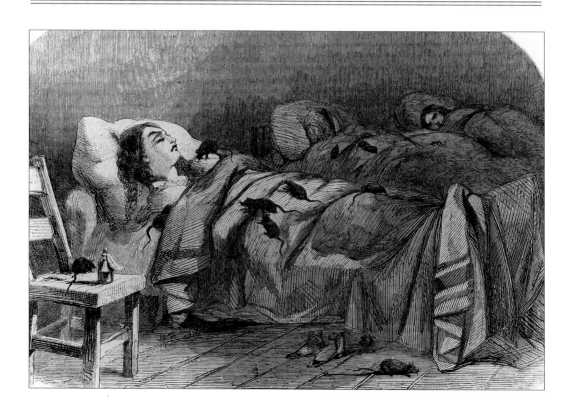

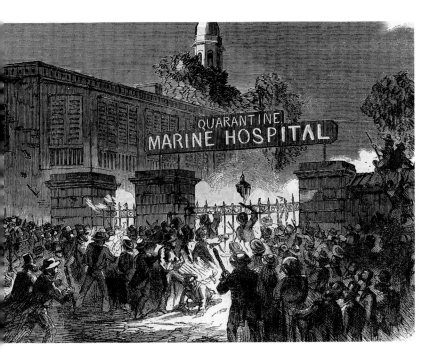

In 1857, New York State constructed a quarantine hospital at Seguines' Point, Staten Island. Residents protested, fearing the spread of both yellow fever and smallpox. Staten Island, then a leading port, experienced a sharp decline in revenue as ships bypassed the city. When a governor's special commission delayed an investigative report, residents set fire to and destroyed the hospital on September 1, 1858.

Walter Reed, one of the most famous names in American medicine and public health. The commission recommended the establishment of diagnostic laboratories in army camps. These labs confirmed that sick soldiers really were suffering from typhoid and not from some other illness.

The next step was to determine how typhoid was infecting the soldiers. The commission did not have to look far. Infected soldiers entering the camps from elsewhere had plenty of opportunity to spread infection, because hygiene in the camps was wretched. Human waste lay scattered on the ground outside latrines. There, flies could pick up disease-causing microbes and carry them into

Religious nursing orders, particularly the Sisters of Charity, visited the sick in their homes. The first American nondenominational visiting nurse service was established in New York City in 1877, in Boston and Philadelphia in 1886, and in Chicago in 1889. These associations, supported by contributions, employed trained nurses chiefly for the care of the sick in their homes. Visiting nurses also taught basic hygiene and sanitation. At the turn of the 20th century, New York's Lower East Side was a blend of nationalities living in overcrowded tenements where the sick often lay unattended. Death rates in this area were among the highest in the city. The photograph shows a visiting nurse in New York City taking a shortcut over the tenement roofs in 1908.

kitchens and mess halls. The link between latrines, flies, food, and typhoid became obvious after lime was scattered around latrines to disinfect them. Afterward, soldiers could see where flies crawling on food had left behind tiny trails of lime.

Corrective measures were easy to implement and had immediate effect. Better latrines improved sanitation in the camps. Lime was

The overall mortality rate due to infantile paralysis (polio) was small. But the disease was deeply feared because it became the leading crippler of children. In a great outpouring of public support for scientific research, millions of American families volunteered to participate in the 1954 trials of the Salk vaccine. Neither doctors, teachers, parents, nor children knew whether the child received the vaccine or a placebo. Pandemonium swept the nation when on April 12, 1955, epidemiologists at the University of Michigan announced the results showing that the vaccine worked.

used extensively for disinfecting. Screens were installed on mess-hall windows to keep flies out. The results were impressive. Between 1898 and 1899, the death rate in army camps dropped from more than 800 per 100,000 to only about 100 per 100,000.

Typhoid and many other diseases were effectively controlled through vigorous public health measures in the final years of the 19th century and the first decades of the 20th. The result was a healthier, happier, and more productive nation. Every dollar spent on public health projects yielded a vast payoff in improved health and productivity.

Not all contagious disease was conquered, nor did every community benefit to the same extent from public health initiatives.

Dept. of Public Health, Div. of Sanitation F. No. 6

CARRIER OF
DIPHTHERIA

KEEP OUT OF THIS HOUSE

By Order of BOARD OF HEALTH

HEALTH OFFICER

Any person removing this card without authority is liable to prosecution

Diphtheria was a communicable disease for which little could be done. During the 1890s, a widespread epidemic swept through the United States, ravaging cities and rural areas alike. While many deaths went unreported, it is estimated that more than 45,000 New York City residents died from diphtheria between 1870 and 1900. Despite this high mortality rate, the city made virtually no public provisions for the sick. Most diphtheria patients were treated at home. Public health departments required a quarantine notice to be posted on entrance doors. This diptheria poster was used in San Francisco around 1915.

But the pestilential American cities of 1800 had become, by the early 1900s, vastly cleaner and much safer from epidemic disease. Furthermore, American society now had adequate institutions—scientific, medical, and political—both to head off epidemics before they occurred and to cope with any epidemics that developed.

In only about half a century, the United States had built a public health infrastructure that extended from federal offices in the nation's capital all the way down to screens on mess-hall windows in far-flung army camps. Few societies ever have transformed themselves so thoroughly, so successfully, and in so short a time.

THE PROFESSIONALIZATION OF MEDICINE

BETWEEN 1800 AND 1900, THE MEDICAL PROFESSION IN America transformed society—and itself—in ways that would have seemed unbelievable at the beginning of the 19th century. The late 19th century witnessed dramatic advances in medical knowledge, education, and practice. These achievements yielded amazing results, both for the individual patient and for public health in general.

Therapeutics changed on a vast scale in the 19th century. For example, the gory practice of bleeding a patient—draining off large quantities of blood in the belief that this enhanced prospects for recovery—went out of favor. As that therapy might indicate, the patient of 1800 was probably in as much danger from physicians and their "remedies" as from any disease that the patient may have suffered. The patient of 1900 was by no means totally free of misguided and potentially dangerous therapies, but on balance had good reason to see doctors and hospitals as agents of probable healing.

Elizabeth Garrett Anderson (1836–1917) became the first woman to practice medicine in Great Britain, in 1870. She trained as a nurse and attended lectures given to medical students at London's Middlesex Hospital until the male students insisted on her leaving. Unsuccessful in all her applications for university courses, she studied privately with medical professors. After qualifying as a midwife, Anderson ran a dispensary for women. Dispensaries were charitable institutions where medical advice was usually given for free. Determined to become a physician, she took her final 45 medical examinations in Paris. With this certificate and her midwife experience, she was allowed to practice medicine. Opposed and lampooned in the beginning, Anderson eventually became a distinguished member of the British Medical Association.

The American hospital developed rapidly in the latter 1800s, from a dismal warehouse for the dying to a well-designed, well-staffed, and efficiently operated institution that offered hope, not despair, to the suffering. According to popular belief, the patient who entered a hospital in 1820 was almost as good as dead. Seventy-five years later, a hospital stay was still cause for concern but no longer seemed equivalent to a sentence of death. Indeed, for some wealthy patients, hospital visits came to be almost fashionable by the start of the 20th century.

Physicians in the early 19th century were poorly educated, disorganized, politically powerless, and scorned by large segments of society. By the century's end, they were well trained, knowledgeable, widely respected, and able to command considerable political power, thanks in part to new professional organizations.

The therapeutics, pharmacopoeia, and medical technology of 1800 appeared to be little advanced over Roman days. By 1900, a vast new number of therapies, medical technologies, and medications had emerged. Serums and vaccines had made many diseases less threatening. Old instruments such as the stethoscope and the clinical thermometer had been refined, and new ones such as X-ray machines had been invented. Etiology, the science of the origins of disease, underwent a revolution in the 19th century, notably in connection with microbiology, which established bacterial causes for some of the ancient enemies of humankind, including tuberculosis, typhoid fever, and diphtheria.

The relationship between the state and the medical profession also changed radically in the 19th century. The practitioner of the early part of the century operated independently of the state. The government did not try to regulate his practice, and he in turn did

Many attempts had been made to build a "horseless carriage" run by steam, electricity, alcohol, or some other fuel. After a series of experiments with a gasoline engine, the automobile became commercially feasible about 1903. Within seven years, some 60 companies were producing cars. This photograph, taken around 1908, is captioned: "The Busy City Doctor who has Many Calls to Make."

not look to the government for special protection or guidance. A much closer relationship between government and the medical profession developed in the 19th century. The state saw a need to improve American medicine by setting and enforcing certain standards on medical practice and education. At the same time, many physicians saw advantages in bringing their profession under regulation by public authorities. Such regulation would encourage adherence to set standards of education and practice, with long-term benefits for physicians and patients alike.

Among the many changes were the imposition of licensing on physicians and the reform of medical schools. Medical education early in the century was unregulated, shoddy, and in many ways dangerous. Many so-called medical schools were operated mainly for profit, so that virtually anyone, no matter how poorly qualified, might acquire a diploma for an appropriate fee. Moreover, the graduate of such a school could embark on the practice of medicine with essentially no official or professional scrutiny. Licensing and medical school reform changed that sad situation. Requiring a license to practice medicine eliminated many quacks and incompetents from the field, while upgrading medical school curricula improved the quality of the trainees entering medical practice.

Professional relationships within the medical community changed too. In the 19th century, medicine ceased to be a pack of ruthlessly competing practitioners and became more of a professional fraternity, characterized by reciprocal courtesies and mutual respect. Doctors recognized that even if they did compete for patients to a certain extent, physicians as a group had many common interests and goals that would be served best by a unified professional organization capable of representing doctors as a class. This change in attitude

The radiology room at an Oklahoma hospital in 1903.

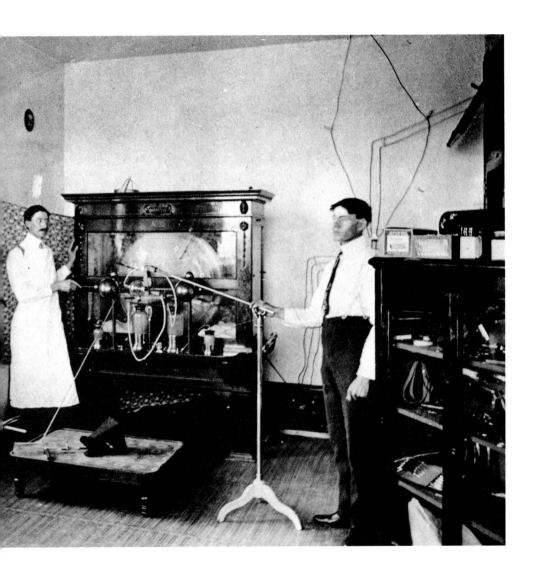

The discovery of X rays by Wilhelm Röntgen in 1895 had a revolutionary impact on surgery and medical research. Almost immediately, physicians recognized the unique value of the X ray in diagnosis and therapy. In addition to showing broken or deformed bones, the shadows revealed other abnormalities, bringing rational diagnosis to the practice of medicine. X-ray facilities in hospitals and offices became centers of diagnostic activity. Tuberculosis, for example, became detectable early, and cancers were found at stages when they could be surgically removed. This engraving shows one of the earliest X-ray machines in use.

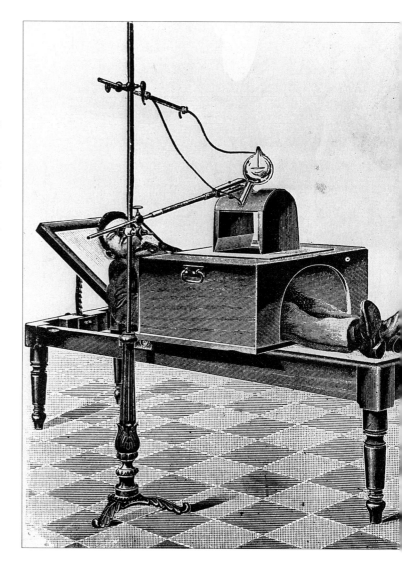

helped make possible the rise of what we call the modern medical establishment, as represented by the powerful American Medical Association and other such organizations.

While the profession of medicine became better organized in the 19th century, individual doctors' practices became more efficient and effective. The rise of the modern hospital allowed doctors to develop a hospital-based practice that made far better use of time and other resources than was possible for the old-fashioned general practitioner, who had to spend much of his time traveling from one patient's home to another in the days when most health care took place at home rather than in a hospital. The new era of hospital-based health care let doctors see greater numbers of patients in a given period.

The economic status of physicians improved in the 19th century. This improvement owed much to hospital-based practice and its efficiencies. More patients meant increased revenues. Furthermore, improvements in the professional reputation of physicians contributed to higher incomes for doctors. As doctors became respected for their skills and training, the public became more willing to pay—in some cases handsomely—for a physician's services. In a few short decades, medicine thus advanced from an underpaid profession in generally low esteem to a highly remunerative and honored line of work.

Improvements in the care of individual patients accompanied advances in public health care. Although early efforts to improve public health were largely the work of voluntary societies, the state and federal governments moved quickly in the late 19th century to support aggressive public health measures. The results were dramatic and immediate. Where public health efforts eliminated

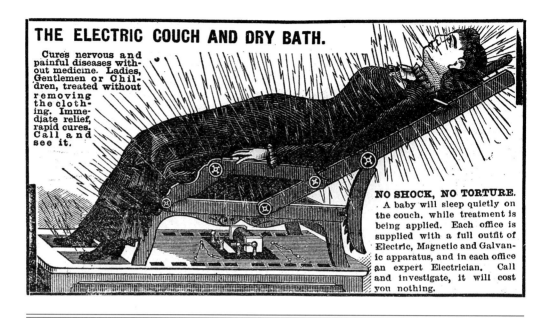

The use of electricity in quack medical devices proliferated at the end of the 19th century. Schemers built complex gadgets, each promising a more miraculous cure. One contraption, the oscilloclast, allegedly produced electric vibrations at the same rate as every known disease. Just set the dials to the proper frequency and any ailment could be cured! Quack electrical devices were advertised in leading magazines, claiming "Electricity is the greatest power on earth," "It puts life and force into whatever it touches," "Gives relief to rheumatism, backaches, kidney, liver, and bladder troubles," "A wonderful discovery," "Joy to invalids!" Magazines of the 1890s were filled with ads for "magnetic cures," "electromagnetic wristbands," "electric belts"—plus an endless variety of electric pads, bracelets, head caps, corsets, combs, and an assortment of machines to transmit current to an ailing body. In recent decades, the Food and Drug Administration has waged an increasingly vigorous and successful campaign against such quackery.

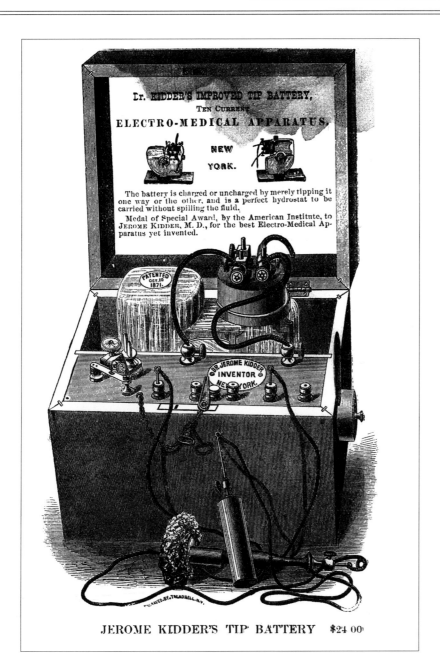

JEROME KIDDER'S TIP BATTERY $24 00

Until the mid-19th century, dentistry was the province of anyone who decided to practice it—regular medical doctors, barber-surgeons, and self-appointed tooth-pullers. The first dental school in the world was the Baltimore College of Dental Surgery, founded in 1839. The 1870 census listed about 10,000 dentists in the United States, but only 1,000 were graduates of a school. Eventually, the specialization of dentistry, with its complex techniques, completely separated from traditional medical practice.

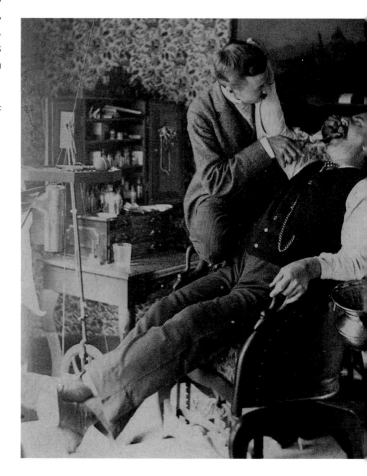

or diminished sources of epidemic disease, epidemics either vanished or at least became less devastating. Government participation was essential here, because many public health efforts were so broad in geographic area and the range and number of institutions affected that only governments had the resources and authority to implement such plans.

The success of public health measures in 19th-century America demonstrated the value of scientific research in public health practices. The conquest of bacterially caused epidemics, for example, owed its success in part to the work of pioneering bacteriologists who established the link between microbes and illness. Without that knowledge, successful public health measures would have been difficult, if not impossible. Public health authorities also learned the importance of modern technology in identifying and controlling infectious agents. For that reason, states started maintaining special, up-to-date bacteriological laboratories to monitor food and water for disease-causing microbes.

The story of 19th-century American medicine, of course, does not consist entirely of triumphs. Social prejudices continued to work against certain elements of society, notably the poor and various ethnic minorities. Prejudice against women in medicine discouraged them from entering medical school and probably deprived the medical community of many highly effective, well-trained, and sympathetic healers. Such practitioners are invaluable at any time, but would have been especially so in the 19th century, when all too many physicians appear to have had a decidedly cold and heartless attitude toward patients.

For all the improvements in therapeutics during the 19th century, health care continued to suffer from a peculiar narrowness of concern on the part of physicians treating disease. A constricted, "scientific" view of humans as mechanisms encouraged doctors to view their patients almost as clockwork devices to be repaired and then returned to service. If a lung or kidney was the problem, then fix it and be done with it—that was the attitude of many doctors. More sensitive and sympathetic doctors would have understood that treating the whole patient, by taking into consideration all the organ systems involved in an illness as well as the patient's emotional state and attitude toward the sickness, would have yielded better results. It would be some time, however, before whole-patient therapy became a standard part of medical education and practice.

Perhaps the most basic change in medical care in the 19th century was, so to speak, a change of venue. Early in the century, most health care in America occurred at home. By the end of the century, health care had been largely removed from the home and entrusted to professionals in special institutions outside the home. The patient was removed from the familiar domestic setting and hauled into a bleak and alien environment where his or her care was placed in the hands of strangers. This transition was unsettling and caused tremendous stress. Although hospitals could provide many therapies that home care could not, the impersonal environment of hospitals did not work entirely in the patient's favor. Even today, after decades of experience, balancing the need for personalized care with the exigencies of hospital treatment is difficult. How much harder it must have been for doctors and patients of the late 19th century!

A more subtle, but equally important, change in health care involved its separation from religion. In many cases, early hospitals were also religious institutions. The rise of the modern, purely secular hospital removed the religious and moral influence of earlier times and with it an important element of health care, especially where the dying patient was concerned.

In the early 19th century, doctors and nurses tended to share with the patient and his or her family a certain set of traditional beliefs concerning life after death. Preparing for death, with those beliefs in mind, was part of health care in terminal cases. By the late 19th century, however, that religious aspect of health care was disappearing fast. This trend has continued in the 20th century. The despiritualization of modern health care has tended to leave the dying patient alone, without spiritual guidance, at the moment of death and just before. Some observers might say that this is the saddest legacy of 19th-century health care.

FURTHER READING

Bordley, James, and A. McGehee Harvey. *Two Centuries of American Medicine*. Philadelphia: Saunders, 1976.

Lyons, Albert, and R. Joseph Petrucelli. *Medicine: An Illustrated History*. New York: Abrams, 1978.

Morantz-Sanchez, Regina. *Sympathy and Science: Women Physicians in American Medicine*. New York: Oxford University Press, 1985.

Rosenberg, Charles. *The Care of Strangers: The Rise of America's Hospital System*. New York: Basic Books, 1987.

Shryock, Richard. *Medicine in America: Historical Essays*. Baltimore: Johns Hopkins Press, 1966.

Starr, Paul. *The Social Transformation of American Medicine*. New York: Basic Books, 1987.

INDEX

PICTURE CREDITS

DAVID RITCHIE is the author of numerous nonfiction books, including *The Computer Pioneers,* a history of early electronic computers, and the *Encyclopedia of Earthquakes and Volcanoes.* He lives in Baltimore, Maryland.

FRED ISRAEL is Professor of History at the City College of New York. His most recent work, in collaboration with Arthur M. Schlesinger, Jr., is *Running for President: The Candidates and Their Images.*

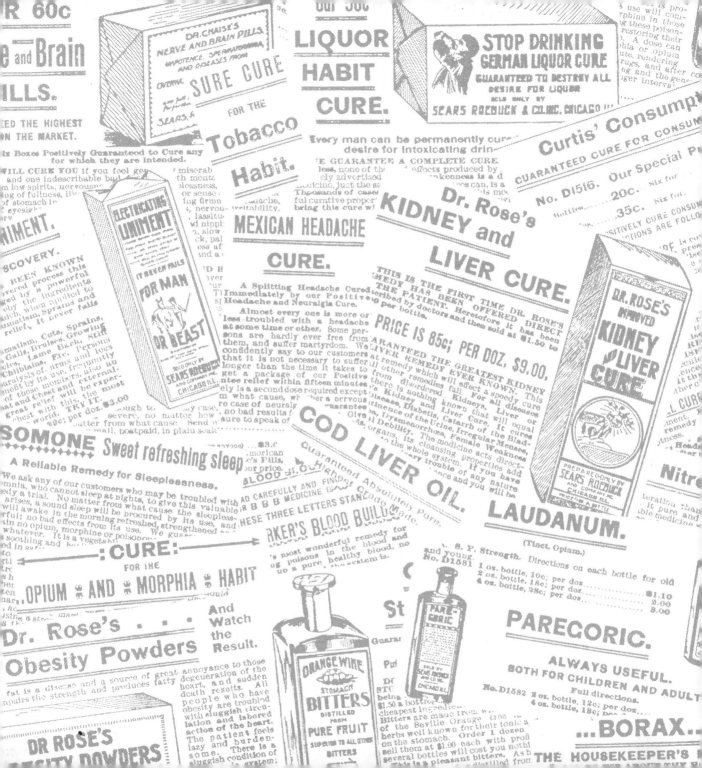